The Lord's Prayer
Leader Guide

THE LORD'S PRAYER
THE MEANING AND POWER
OF THE PRAYER JESUS TAUGHT

978-1-7910-2125-2 *Hardcover*
978-1-7910-2126-9 *eBook*
978-1-7910-2127-6 *Large Print*

DVD
978-1-7910-2130-6

Leader Guide
978-1-7910-2128-3
978-1-7910-2129-0 eBook

Find out more about
Adam Hamilton's
children's book
*The Most Important
Prayer of All:
Stella Learns the
Lord's Prayer* at
**AdamHamilton.com/
LordsPrayer**

Also by Adam Hamilton

24 Hours That Changed the World

Christianity and World Religions

Creed

Enough

Faithful

Final Words from the Cross

Forgiveness

Half Truths

Incarnation

John

Making Sense of the Bible

Not a Silent Night

Seeing Gray in a World
of Black and White

Simon Peter

The Journey

The Walk

The Way

Words of Life

Why?

For more information, visit www.AdamHamilton.com.

ADAM HAMILTON

Author of *Creed, The Walk,* and *The Journey*

THE LORD'S PRAYER

THE MEANING AND POWER OF THE PRAYER JESUS TAUGHT

LEADER GUIDE

by Mike Poteet

Abingdon Press | Nashville

The Lord's Prayer
The Meaning and Power of the Prayer Jesus Taught
Leader Guide

Copyright © 2021 Abingdon Press
All rights reserved.

No part of this work may be reproduced or transmitted in any form or by any means, electronic or mechanical, including photocopying and recording, or by any information storage or retrieval system, except as may be expressly permitted by the 1976 Copyright Act, the 1998 Digital Millennium Copyright Act, or in writing from the publisher. Requests for permission can be addressed to Rights and Permissions, The United Methodist Publishing House, 810 12th Avenue South, Nashville TN 37203 or e-mailed to permissions@abingdonpress.com.

978-1-7910-2128-3

Scripture quotations unless noted otherwise are from the Common English Bible. Copyright © 2011 by the Common English Bible. All rights reserved. Used by permission. www.CommonEnglishBible.com.

21 22 23 24 25 26 27 28 29 30 — 10 9 8 7 6 5 4 3 2 1
MANUFACTURED IN THE UNITED STATES OF AMERICA

CONTENTS

TO THE LEADER

In *The Lord's Prayer*, Adam Hamilton invites readers to consider closely the words and themes of the prayer Jesus taught his disciples. "The prayer is meant by Jesus," he writes, "to shape our lives and, through us, to shape and change the world."

This guide is designed to help leaders of adult Christian education groups to discuss and learn from Hamilton's book together. It will prove most valuable when used as a supplement to rather than a replacement for Hamilton's book.

Its six sessions follow the same structure as Hamilton's book:

Session 1—Our Father, Who Art in Heaven, Hallowed Be Thy Name

Participants will compare and contrast the two versions of the Lord's Prayer found in the New Testament, consider what it means to address God as "Our Father," and identify practical ways to "hallow" God's name.

Session 2—Whose Will Be Done?

Participants will consider Jesus as a model of discerning and doing God's will and will discuss ways they and their congregations can do God's will in the world today.

7

Session 3–Our Daily Bread

Participants will take an honest look at how much of their eating is essential, examine the biblical story of the wilderness manna as context for the Lord's Prayer, and determine ways they can answer other people's prayers for both physical and spiritual bread.

Session 4–Forgive...As We Forgive

Participants will define what *forgiveness* does and does not mean and will interpret two of Jesus's parables as they seek ways to extend forgiveness to others.

Session 5–And Lead Us, Not into Temptation

Participants will explore two key biblical stories about temptation (the humans and the serpent in Eden, and the temptations Jesus faced in the wilderness) and consider the "armor of God" in Ephesians 6 as an image for withstanding temptations.

Session 6–For THINE Is the Kingdom, Power, and Glory

Participants will examine the importance of praising God in prayer and consider how the closing doxology in the Lord's Prayer shapes Christian attitudes toward power and glory.

HOW TO FACILITATE THIS STUDY

This study makes use of the following components:

- *The Lord's Prayer*, by Adam Hamilton.
- This *Leader Guide*.
- *The Lord's Prayer DVD*, or access to the streaming video sessions via Amplify Media (www.amplifymedia.com).
- The Bible. A variety of translations are both allowable and desirable in your small group. Multiple translations allow you to compare wording and open the possibility for new insights into the text. Some great translations include the

Common English Bible (CEB), New Revised Standard Version (NRSV), and New International Version (NIV).

Each session should take approximately 45-60 minutes to complete and consists of the following segments:

- **Session Goals:** Describes the objectives of this week's lesson.
- **Biblical Foundations:** Contains the key Scripture texts for this week's lesson.
- **Opening (5-15 minutes):** Gather the group together, introduce the main ideas for this lesson with a brief discussion or activity, then open with prayer.
- **Discussion (30-45 minutes):** Discuss the week's chapter of The Lord's Prayer by Adam Hamilton, using the videos, key Scripture texts, and discussion questions that are provided in this guide.
- **Closing (5 minutes):** Invite the group to raise any prayer concerns or reasons for thanksgiving, then close with prayer.

HELPFUL HINTS

Preparing for Each Session

- Carefully read the corresponding chapter of Adam Hamilton's The Lord's Prayer.
- Prayerfully read the session's Biblical Foundations, noting questions and issues you need or want to study further. Consult trusted biblical references for more information.
- Gather Bibles for participants (and/or slides of the session's Biblical Foundations for screen sharing purposes), newsprint, or markerboard.
- Review the discussion questions for the session and select the ones you want to spend the most time with in your

group. Be prepared, however, to adjust the session as group members interact and as questions arise. Prepare carefully, but allow space for the Holy Spirit to move in and through the group members and through you as facilitator.

- Prepare the space where the group will meet so that the space will enhance the learning process. Ideally, group members should be seated around a table or in a circle so that all can see one another.

Shaping the Learning Environment

- Create a climate of openness, encouraging group members to participate as they feel comfortable.
- Remember that some people will jump right in with answers and comments, while others need time to process what is being discussed.
- If you notice that some group members seem never to be able to enter the conversation, ask them if they have thoughts to share. Give everyone a chance to talk, but keep the conversation moving. Moderate to prevent a few individuals from doing all the talking.
- Communicate the importance of group discussions and group exercises.
- If no one answers at first during discussions, do not be afraid of silence. Count silently to ten, then say something such as, "Would anyone like to go first?" If no one responds, venture an answer yourself and ask for comments.
- Model openness as you share with the group. Group members will follow your example. If you limit your sharing to a surface level, others will follow suit.

- Encourage multiple answers or responses before moving on to the next question.
- Ask "Why?" or "Why do you believe that?" or "Can you say more about that?" to help continue a discussion and give it greater depth.
- Affirm others' responses with comments such as "Great" or "Thanks" or "Good insight"—especially if it's the first time someone has spoken during the group session.
- Monitor your own contributions. If you are doing most of the talking, back off so that you do not train the group to listen rather than speak up.
- Remember that you do not have to have all the answers. Your job is to keep the discussion going and encourage participation.

Managing the Session

- Honor the time schedule. If a session is running longer than expected, get consensus from the group before continuing beyond the agreed-upon ending time.
- Involve group members in various aspects of the group session, such as saying prayers or reading the Scripture.
- As always in discussions that may involve personal sharing, confidentiality is essential. Group members should never pass along stories that have been shared in the group. Remind the group members at each session: confidentiality is crucial to the success of this study.

As an option for closing each session, consider choosing a musical setting of the Lord's Prayer to listen to and/or sing together. Many composers have set the Lord's Prayer to music, in many styles; consider using different settings, from a variety of cultural backgrounds, for each of your six sessions to emphasize how the Lord's Prayer belongs to all Christians.

All scriptural quotations in the guide come from the Common English Bible.

Thank you for leading your group in this study of the Lord's Prayer—and *The Lord's Prayer* by Adam Hamilton! May your shared readings, discussions, and prayers shape your praying and your faithful living in new and exciting ways.

ADAPTING FOR VIRTUAL SMALL GROUP SESSIONS

Meeting online is a great option for a number of situations. During a time of a public-health hazard, such as the COVID-19 pandemic, online meetings are a welcome opportunity for people to converse while seeing each other's faces. Online meetings can also expand the "neighborhood" of possible group members, because people can log in from just about anywhere in the world. This also gives those who do not have access to transportation or who prefer not to travel at certain times of day the chance to participate.

The guidelines below will help you lead an effective and enriching group study using an online video conferencing platform such as Zoom, Webex, Google Meet, Microsoft Teams, or another virtual meeting platform of your choice.

BASIC FEATURES FOR VIRTUAL MEETINGS

There are many choices for videoconferencing platforms. You may have personal experience and comfort using a particular service, or your church may have a subscription that will influence your choice. Whichever option you choose, it is recommended that you use a platform that supports the following features:

- **Synchronous video and audio:** Your participants can see and speak to each other live, in real time. Participants have the ability to turn their video off and on, and to mute and unmute their audio.

- **Chat:** Your participants can send text messages to the whole group or individuals from within the virtual meeting. Participants can put active hyperlinks (i.e., "clickable" internet addresses) into the chat for other participants' convenience.
- **Screen Sharing:** Participants can share the contents of their screen with other participants (the meeting host's permission may be required).
- **Video Sharing:** Participants (or the host) can share videos and computer audio via screen share, so that all participants can view the videos each week.
- **Breakout Rooms:** Meeting hosts can automatically or manually send participants into virtual smaller groups and can determine whether the rooms end automatically after a set period of time. Hosts can communicate with all breakout rooms. *This feature is useful if your group is large, or if you wish to break into smaller teams of two or three for certain activities. If you have a smaller group, this feature may not be necessary.*

Check with your pastor or director of discipleship to see if your church has a preferred platform or an account with one or more of these platforms that you might use. In most instances, only the host will need to be signed in to the account; others can participate without being registered.

Zoom, Webex, Google Meet, and Microsoft Teams all offer free versions of their platform, which you can use if your church doesn't have an account. However, there may be some restrictions (for instance, Zoom's free version limits meetings to 45 minutes). Check each platform's website to be sure you are aware of any such restrictions before you sign up.

Once you have selected a platform, familiarize yourself with all of its features and controls so that you can facilitate virtual meetings comfortably. The platform's website will have lists of features and helpful tutorials; often third-party sites will have useful information or instructions as well.

There are additional features on many that help play your video more effectively. In Zoom, for example, as you click the "share screen" option and see the screen showing your different windows, check at the bottom of that window to choose "optimize for video clips" and "share audio." These ensure that your group hears the audio and that, when using a clip, the video resolution is compressed to fit the bandwidth that you have.

In addition to videoconferencing software, it is also advisable to have access to slide-creation software such as Microsoft PowerPoint or Google Slides. These can be used to prepare easy slides for screen-sharing to display discussion questions, quotes from the study book, or Scripture passages. If you don't have easy access to these, you can create a document and share it—but make sure the print size is easy to read.

VIDEO SHARING

For a video-based study, it's important to be able to screen-share your videos so that all participants can view them in your study session. The good news is, whether you have the videos on DVD or streaming files, it is possible to play them in your session.

All of the videoconferencing platforms mentioned above support screen-sharing videos. Some have specific requirements for assuring that sound will play clearly in addition to the videos. Follow your videoconferencing platform instructions carefully, and test the video sharing in advance to be sure it works.

If you wish to screen-share a DVD video, you may need to use a different media player. Some media players will not allow you to share your screen when you play copyright-protected DVDs. VLC is a free media player that is safe and easy to use. To try this software, download at videolan.org/VLC.

What about copyright? DVDs like those you use for group study are meant to be used in a group setting "real time." That is, whether you meet in person, online, or in a hybrid setting, Abingdon Press encourages use of your DVD or streaming video.

What is allowed: Streaming an Abingdon DVD over Zoom, Teams, or similar platform during a small group session.

What is not allowed: Posting video of a published DVD study to social media or YouTube for later viewing.

If you have any questions about permissions and copyright, email permissions@abingdonpress.com.

Amplify Media. The streaming subscription platform Amplify Media makes it easy to share streaming videos for groups. When your church has an Amplify subscription, your group members can sign on and have access to the video sessions. With access, they may watch the video on their own ahead of your group meeting, watch the streaming video during your group meeting, or view it again after the meeting. Thousands of videos are on AmplifyMedia.com making it easy to watch anytime, anywhere, and on any device from phones and tablets to Smart TVs and desktops.

Visit AmplifyMedia.com to learn more or call 1-800-672-1789, option 4, to hear about the current offers.

COMMUNICATING WITH YOUR GROUP

Clear communication with your small group before and throughout your study is crucial no matter how you meet, but it is doubly important if you are gathering virtually.

Advertising the Study. Be sure to advertise your virtual study on your church's website and/or in its newsletter, as well as any social media that your church uses. Request pastors or other worship leaders to announce it in worship services.

Registration. Encourage people to register for the online study so that you can know all participants and have a way to contact them. Ideally, you will collect an email address for each participant so that you can send them communications and links to your virtual meeting sessions. An event planning tool such as SignUpGenius makes this easy and gives you a database of participants and their email addresses.

Welcome Email. Before your first session, several days in advance, send an email to everyone who has registered for the study, welcoming them to the group, reminding them of the date and time of your first meeting, and including a link to join the virtual meeting. It's also a good idea to include one or two discussion questions to "prime the pump" for reflection and conversation when you gather.

If you have members without internet service, or if they are uncomfortable using a computer and videoconferencing software, let them know they may telephone into the meeting. Provide them the number and let them know that there is usually a unique phone number for each meeting.

Weekly Emails. Send a new email two or three days before each week's session, again including the link to join your virtual meeting and one or two discussion questions to set the stage for discussion. Feel free to use any of the questions in the Leader Guide for this purpose. If you find a particular quote from the book that is especially meaningful, include this as well.

Facebook. Consider creating a private Facebook group for your small group, where you can hold discussion and invite reflection between your weekly meetings. Each week, post one or two quotes from the study book along with a short question for reflection, and invite people to respond in the comments. These questions can come straight from the Leader Guide, and you can revisit the Facebook conversation during your virtual meeting.

You might also consider posting these quotes and questions on your church's main Facebook page, inviting people in your congregation to join the conversation beyond your small group. This can be a great way to involve others in your study, or to let people know about it and invite them to join your next virtual meeting.

DURING YOUR VIRTUAL SESSIONS

During your virtual sessions, follow these tips to be sure you are prepared and that everything runs as smoothly as possible.

Getting Ready

- Familiarize yourself with the controls and features of your videoconferencing platform, using instructions or tutorials available via the platform's website or third-party sites.
- Be sure you are leading the session from a well-lit place in front of a background free from excessive distractions.
- As leader, log into the virtual meeting early. You want to be a good host who is present to welcome participants by name as they arrive. This also gives you time to check how you appear on camera, so that you can make any last-minute adjustments to your lighting and background if needed.

Creating Community Online

- During each session, pay attention to who is speaking and who is not. Because of video and audio lags as well as internet connections of varying quality, some participants may inadvertently speak over each other without realizing they are doing so. As needed, directly prompt specific people to speak if they wish (for example, "Alan, it looked like you were about to say something when Sarah was speaking").
- If your group is especially large, you may want to agree with members on a procedure for being recognized to speak (for example, participants might "raise hands" digitally or type "call on me" in the chat feature).
- Instruct participants to keep their microphones muted during the meeting, so extraneous noise from their location does not interrupt the meeting. This includes

chewing or yawning sounds, which can be embarrassing! When it is time for discussion, participants can unmute themselves.

- Remember some participants may wish to simply observe and listen—do not pressure anyone to speak who does not wish to.
- Always get your group's permission before recording your online sessions. While those who are unable to attend the meeting may appreciate the chance to view it later, respect the privacy of your participants.
- Communicate with your group in between sessions with weekly emails and Facebook posts to spark ongoing discussion.

In challenging times, modern technology has powerful potential to bring God's people together in new and nourishing ways. May such be your experience during this virtual study.

HELP, SUPPORT, AND TUTORIALS

The creators of the most popular virtual meeting platforms have excellent, free resources available online to help you get started using their platform, which teach you everything from how to join a meeting as a participant to how to use the more advanced features like video sharing and breakout rooms. Most of them offer clear written instructions as well as video tutorials and also provide a way to contact the company in case you need additional assistance.

Below are links for five platforms: Zoom, Microsoft Teams, Webex, Google Meet, and GoTo Meeting. If you are using a different platform, go to their website and look for the "Help" or "Resources" page.

Zoom Help Center: https://support.zoom.us/hc/en-us.
Contains a comprehensive collection of resources to help you use the Zoom platform, including quick start guides, video tutorials, articles, and specific sets of instructions on various topics or issues.

Microsoft Teams Help & Learning: https://support.microsoft.com /en-us/teams.

A collection of articles, videos, and instructions on how to use the Microsoft Teams platform. Teams offers a number of features. You are most likely to find the help you need for group meetings by navigating to the "Meetings" page, or by clicking "Microsoft Teams training" under "Explore Microsoft Teams."

Webex Help Center: https://help.webex.com/en-us/.

Contains articles, videos, and other resources to help you use the Webex platform, with everything from joining the meeting to screen-sharing and using a virtual whiteboard.

Google Meet Help: https://support.google.com/meet/.

Contains a list of support topics to help you use the Google Meet platform, in an easy-to-read expandable list that makes it easy to find just what you need.

GoTo Meeting Support: https://support.goto.com/meeting.

Here you'll find links with instructions on various topics to help you use the GoTo Meeting platform.

GENERAL HOW-TO

In addition to these official support pages, there are numerous independent sites online with great, clear instructions on using multiple platforms. Here is one excellent resource:

Nerds Chalk: https://nerdschalk.com/.

This site is easily searchable and contains numerous articles and how-to guides, with clear titles to help you find exactly what you need. Simply search for your chosen platform and/or what you are trying to accomplish, such as "Breakout rooms" or "Zoom screen share," and navigate to the most relevant link.

SESSION 1

OUR FATHER, WHO ART IN HEAVEN, HALLOWED BE THY NAME

SESSION GOALS

Through this session's Scripture readings, discussion, reflection, and prayer, participants will:

- Talk about their experiences with the Lord's Prayer.
- Examine the contexts of Jesus's prayer in the Gospels of Matthew and Luke.
- Consider the significance of calling God "Our Father in heaven."
- Identify practical applications of the first petition in the Lord's Prayer, "Hallowed be thy name."

BIBLICAL FOUNDATIONS

Matthew 6:5-15

[Jesus said,] "When you pray, don't be like hypocrites. They love to pray standing in the synagogues and on the

street corners so that people will see them. I assure you, that's the only reward they'll get. But when you pray, go to your room, shut the door, and pray to your Father who is present in that secret place. Your Father who sees what you do in secret will reward you.

"When you pray, don't pour out a flood of empty words, as the Gentiles do. They think that by saying many words they'll be heard. Don't be like them, because your Father knows what you need before you ask. Pray like this:

Our Father who is in heaven,
uphold the holiness of your name.
Bring in your kingdom
so that your will is done on earth as it's done in heaven.
Give us the bread we need for today.
Forgive us for the ways we have wronged you,
just as we also forgive those who have wronged us.
And don't lead us into temptation,
but rescue us from the evil one.

"If you forgive others their sins, your heavenly Father will also forgive you. But if you don't forgive others, neither will your Father forgive your sins."

Luke 11:1-10

Jesus was praying in a certain place. When he finished, one of his disciples said, "Lord, teach us to pray, just as John taught his disciples."

Jesus told them, "When you pray, say:

'Father, uphold the holiness of your name.
Bring in your kingdom.
Give us the bread we need for today.
Forgive us our sins,
      for we also forgive everyone who has wronged us.
And don't lead us into temptation.'"

He also said to them, "Imagine that one of you has a
friend and you go to that friend in the middle of the night.
Imagine saying, 'Friend, loan me three loaves of bread
because a friend of mine on a journey has arrived and I
have nothing to set before him.' Imagine further that he
answers from within the house, 'Don't bother me. The
door is already locked, and my children and I are in bed.
I can't get up to give you anything.' I assure you, even if he
wouldn't get up and help because of his friendship, he will
get up and give his friend whatever he needs because of his
friend's brashness. And I tell you: Ask and you will receive.
Seek and you will find. Knock and the door will be opened
to you. Everyone who asks, receives. Whoever seeks, finds.
To everyone who knocks, the door is opened."

OPENING YOUR SESSION

Welcome participants. Express your enthusiasm for leading this
study of *The Lord's Prayer* by Adam Hamilton. Talk briefly about what
you hope to gain from the study and invite participants to do the same.
Discuss:

- Adam Hamilton's grandmother taught him the Lord's
  Prayer. How did you first learn the Lord's Prayer?
  With whom, if anyone, in your life do you associate it,
  and why?
- Hamilton states, "No other prayer is more important
  to Christians than this prayer." Do you agree? Why
  or why not?
- Of the Lord's Prayer, Hamilton writes, "We know it, but
  often we don't *know* it. We pray it, but all too often we
  don't actually *pray* it." What does he mean? Do you agree?
  Why or why not?
- When was a time you found the Lord's Prayer especially
  meaningful, and why?

- What questions about the Lord's Prayer, if any, do you
  bring to this study? *(Write responses on newsprint or
  markerboard and keep the list available for reference during
  remaining sessions.)*

Pray aloud this prayer or one in your own words:

*Holy God, as you rule over all in heaven and on earth, so rule our time to-
gether by your Spirit. In our reading, in our discussing, and in our praying,
direct our minds and hearts toward you, that we may praise your glorious
name in all we say and do.* **Amen.**

WATCH *THE LORD'S PRAYER* VIDEO

Play *The Lord's Prayer* video for Session 1 using your DVD player
or stream with Amplify Media. When the session has finished, invite
volunteers to lift up one or two key ideas that stood out in the video.

As you continue your discussion of the Lord's Prayer below, refer
to the video as well as to chapter 1 of Hamilton's book and the Scripture passages.

STUDY MATTHEW'S AND LUKE'S SETTINGS OF THE LORD'S PRAYER

Tell participants the text we know as the Lord's Prayer occurs, in
slightly different forms, in two of the Gospels: Matthew and Luke.
Suggest that reading the prayer in each of its settings can help us better
understand not only it but also prayer in general.

Recruit one or more volunteers to read aloud Matthew 6:5-15.
Discuss:

- What prompts Jesus to give the Lord's Prayer in this
  Scripture?
- A devout Jew, Jesus didn't mention synagogues to criticize
  Jewish prayer in general (verse 5), but to criticize an
  attention-seeking attitude. How does the Lord's Prayer

encourage our attention, when praying, to remain on God where it belongs?

- Jesus also criticized long-winded, meaningless prayers (verse 7). How does the Lord's Prayer help us avoid such prayer?
- Why do you think Jesus elaborates on the prayer's final petition (verses 14-15)?
- Skim the "Sermon on the Mount" (Matthew 5–7), the collection of Jesus's teachings in which Matthew places the Lord's Prayer. What connections can you make between Jesus's prayer and the rest of the "Sermon"?

Recruit one or more volunteers to read aloud Luke 11:1-10. Discuss:

- What prompts Jesus to give the Lord's Prayer in this Scripture?
- What differences between Luke's and Matthew's versions of Jesus's prayer do you notice? What significance, if any, do you find in them?
- What attitudes toward prayer does Jesus teach in the parable immediately following the Lord's Prayer (verses 5-10)? How do they compare with those in Matthew 5?
- Hamilton says the Lord's Prayer, "like all prayer, is less about informing God of things we want or need, and more about shaping our own heart and life." Based on their settings for the Lord's Prayer, how do you imagine Matthew and Luke would respond? Why?

CALLING GOD "OUR FATHER IN HEAVEN"

Lead participants in brainstorming a list of as many names, titles, and/or images for God as they remember from (or can find while browsing) the Bible. When finished, point out, as Hamilton writes, "when Jesus taught his disciples to pray…He taught them to address God as, 'Our Father.'"

Discuss:

- What qualities did this name, "Father," evoke for Jesus? Are they qualities you associate with fathers and father-hood? Why or why not?
- Hamilton wonders whether Jesus's memories of his adoptive father Joseph influenced Jesus's addressing God as Father. Read the following Scripture verses:
  - ◊ Matthew 1:18-25
  - ◊ Matthew 2:13-23
  - ◊ Luke 2:21-24
  - ◊ Luke 2:39-51
- How might Joseph's qualities have influenced Jesus's view of God?
- "Your earthly father is not the pattern for God's father-hood," writes Hamilton, "but *God is the pattern and example of what a father is meant to be.*" How important or helpful do you find this distinction, and why?
- Hamilton states "both fathering and mothering are a part of God's nature and character. " How are fathering and mothering different and alike?
- How does addressing God as "our Father" rather than "my Father" shape our view of God and of other people?
- Hamilton discusses several ways of understanding God's location "in heaven." Which of these do you find most meaningful? most surprising? Why?
- Do you think Jesus's encouragement to pray to God as "Our Father in heaven" is an instruction or an invitation, an obligation or an option? Why? How does the Lord's Prayer help us determine what other names, if any, we can or should use to address God?

HALLOWING THE NAME OF GOD

Review Hamilton's definition of being "hallowed" or holy: It is to be "set apart for God and for God's purposes.... [It] can also mean pure, or that which is wholly different from the ordinary. It can signify something or someone that is cleansed, purified, righteous, or utterly good. Finally, it can mean 'revered or something that inspires awe.'"

Discuss:

- What are we asking God to do when asking God to "hallow" God's name?
- How is this petition related to the commandment in Exodus 20:7 and Deuteronomy 5:11?
- How do you see and hear God's name treated as of great and/or as of no significance in culture? in government? in the church? in your own life?
- Hamilton argues "to pray for God to hallow God's name is to desire that God's name be hallowed... [and to] invite God to use us to hallow God's name." What are some practical and specific ways you are hallowing God's name through the way that you live?
- What does your congregation do, specifically and concretely, to hallow God's name?

CLOSING YOUR SESSION

Ask volunteers to talk about one specific way they plan to hallow God's name before the next session. Be ready to start discussion by sharing your own plan.

Point out Hamilton's discussion of the idea of *ora et labora*, Latin for "pray and work," found on page xvii of the Introduction. Encourage participants to pay attention, in between sessions, for ways their engagement with the Lord's Prayer during this study shapes their own prayer and work.

Close by inviting participants to pray together the version of the Lord's Prayer with which they are most familiar.

Option:

Hamilton mentions the *Didache*, a first- or second-century church document that indicates some early Christians prayed the Lord's Prayer three times daily (9 am, noon, 3 pm). Encourage participants to consider adopting this discipline for the duration of your study—not for praise from other group members or "gold stars" in God's eyes, but to let the Lord's Prayer shape and sustain them.

SESSION 2

WHOSE WILL BE DONE?

SESSION GOALS

Through this session's Scripture readings, discussion, reflection, and prayer, participants will:

- React to and reflect on some commonly heard assertions about God's will.
- Read and discuss two prophetic visions (one from Isaiah, the other from Revelation) of the kingdom of God.
- Contemplate how Jesus modeled seeking and doing God's will, especially as he prayed before his suffering and death.
- Identify practical ways in which they and their congregations do or could "close the gap" between the world as it is and the world as God wills it to be.

BIBLICAL FOUNDATIONS

Luke 22:39-46

> *Jesus left and made his way to the Mount of Olives, as*
> *was his custom, and the disciples followed him. When*

29

he arrived, he said to them, "Pray that you won't give in to temptation." He withdrew from them about a stone's throw, knelt down, and prayed. He said, "Father, if it's your will, take this cup of suffering away from me. However, not my will but your will must be done." Then a heavenly angel appeared to him and strengthened him. He was in anguish and prayed even more earnestly. His sweat became like drops of blood falling on the ground. When he got up from praying, he went to the disciples. He found them asleep, overcome by grief. He said to them, "Why are you sleeping? Get up and pray so that you won't give in to temptation."

Isaiah 2:2-5

In the days to come
> *the mountain of the LORD's house*
> *will be the highest of the mountains.*
> *It will be lifted above the hills;*
> > *peoples will stream to it.*

Many nations will go and say,
"Come, let's go up to the LORD's mountain,
> *to the house of Jacob's God*
> > *so that he may teach us his ways*
> > *and we may walk in God's paths."*

Instruction will come from Zion;
> *the LORD's word from Jerusalem.*

God will judge between the nations,
> *and settle disputes of mighty nations.*

Then they will beat their swords into iron plows
> *and their spears into pruning tools.*

Nation will not take up sword against nation;
> *they will no longer learn how to make war.*

Come, house of Jacob,
> *let's walk by the Lord's light.*

Revelation 21:1-5

> *Then I saw a new heaven and a new earth, for the former heaven and the former earth had passed away, and the sea was no more. I saw the holy city, New Jerusalem, coming down out of heaven from God, made ready as a bride beautifully dressed for her husband. I heard a loud voice from the throne say, "Look! God's dwelling is here with humankind. He will dwell with them, and they will be his peoples. God himself will be with them as their God. He will wipe away every tear from their eyes. Death will be no more. There will be no mourning, crying, or pain anymore, for the former things have passed away." Then the one seated on the throne said, "Look! I'm making all things new."*

ADDITIONAL PREPARATION FOR SESSION 2

- Gather artwork depicting Jesus praying in Gethsemane (from books or properly vetted online sources).
- Write the three discussion questions from the section "Glimpsing the Kingdom in Scripture" on newsprint or markerboard. (If meeting online, put them on a slide so you can share them in your online meeting via screen share, or type them in the platform's chat feature.)

OPENING YOUR SESSION

Welcome participants. Ask volunteers who attended the previous session to talk briefly about how insights they gained from it have been shaping their prayer and work (*ora et labora*).

Consult the list of questions about the Lord's Prayer your group made in Session 1. Ask whether participants, as a result of the previous session, have answers or insights about these questions to offer the group.

Ask participants to write their reactions to each statement below using a 1–5 scale (1=strongly agree; 2=mostly agree; 3=neither agree nor disagree; 4=mostly disagree; 5=strongly disagree).

- Everything happens for a reason.
- God has a plan for your life.
- It's difficult to know God's will.
- God is in control.
- God's ways are not our ways.

Ask participants to which statement, if any, they reacted most strongly, and why. (If needed, assure participants there are no "right answers" in this activity; not all Christians would or must react the same way.)

Adam Hamilton quotes Father Daniel Harrington as saying God's will is the "central concern" of the Lord's Prayer. In this session, your group will explore this concern.

Pray aloud this prayer or one in your own words:

Sovereign God, who created and rules over all: Fix our hearts and minds in this time together on the day when your will shall be done on earth as in heaven, and by your Spirit make us so long for its dawning that we live every day in more faithful obedience to your Son, our Savior, Jesus Christ. **Amen.**

WATCH *THE LORD'S PRAYER* VIDEO

Play *The Lord's Prayer* video for Session 2 using your DVD player or stream with Amplify Media. When the session has finished, invite volunteers to lift up one or two key ideas that stood out in the video.

As you continue your discussion of the Lord's Prayer below, refer to the video as well as to chapter 2 of Hamilton's book and the Scripture passages.

GLIMPSING THE KINGDOM IN SCRIPTURE

Read aloud from *The Lord's Prayer*: "You cannot fully understand Jesus, what he taught, stood for, and incarnated without understanding the kingdom of heaven" or kingdom (rule, reign) of God. "What are we praying when we pray for God's kingdom to come? We are praying for God's will to be done on earth as it is in heaven."

Form two groups of participants. (If meeting remotely or in a hybrid format, utilize your platform's breakout rooms feature.) Ask one group to read and discuss Isaiah 2:2-5, and the other to read and discuss Revelation 21:1-5. Note that these Scriptures are only two of many descriptions and visions of God's kingdom in the Bible. Have each group use these questions (on newsprint or marker-board, screen-shared, or typed in the chat prior to breakout rooms) to spark discussion:

- How does this Scripture show God's will being done on earth?
- What connections can you draw between this Scripture and how Jesus embodied the Kingdom?
- What actions does or might this vision of God's coming kingdom inspire you and/or your congregation to take now?

Allow 5–10 minutes for discussion, then invite a volunteer from each group to report on highlights of their group's conversation.

"THY WILL, NOT MINE, BE DONE"

Show participants several artistic depictions of Jesus praying in Gethsemane. (Simply searching that phrase in Google Images will return many options.) Discuss:

- How alike and/or different are these images?

33

- Which of these images most attracts your attention, and why?
- What does Jesus appear to be feeling or thinking in these images?

Recruit a volunteer to read aloud Luke 22:39-46. Discuss:

- What is the will of God about which Jesus prays?
- Why does praying about it cause him to struggle?
- How well or poorly do the pictures we looked at communicate Jesus's anguish over God's will? Why?
- When else in his life and ministry did Jesus model seeking and doing God's will?
- When was a time you struggled to know and do God's will?
- This story contrasts doing God's will with yielding to temptation. When do you feel tempted to disobey or disregard God's will? How do you handle those temptations? How does or could your church help you deal with them?

CLOSING THE GAP BETWEEN EARTH AND HEAVEN

"Doing God's will and living this prayer," writes Hamilton, "involves closing the gap between the world as it is and the world as it is supposed to be."

Discuss:

- How do we pray for God's will to be done without resigning ourselves to the "fatalism" Hamilton rejects—the idea that "God will do what God wants to do"?
- Different people have different ideas about the way the world is "supposed to be." How should Christians discern the way God wants the world to be?

- How do or how ought Christians handle disagreements with each other about practical implications of praying to be agents of God's will (whom to vote for, which political causes to support, and so on)?
- Hamilton introduces us to two people he knows, Bobbi Jo Reed and James McGinnis, whom he believes help close the gap between the world as it is and as it should be. Who is such a person you know? How does she or he embody God's kingdom?
- How can or how could the vision of God's coming kingdom help you and your congregation find common ground and common cause with non-Christians for the purpose of more faithfully doing God's will?

CLOSING YOUR SESSION

Ask volunteers to talk about one specific way they plan to do God's will on earth as it is done in heaven before the next session. Be ready to start discussion by sharing your own plan.

Close by inviting participants to pray together the version of the Lord's Prayer with which they are most familiar.

SESSION 3

OUR DAILY BREAD
SESSION GOALS

Through this session's Scripture readings, discussion, reflection, and prayer, participants will:

- Estimate and reflect on how much of their eating is essential eating.
- Consider what the story of God giving manna in the desert can teach God's people today.
- Reflect on what it means to call Jesus "the Bread of Life."
- Identify specific ways to be God's answer to other people's prayers for bread.

BIBLICAL FOUNDATIONS

Exodus 16:14-21

> When the layer of dew lifted, there on the desert surface
> were thin flakes, as thin as frost on the ground. When the
> Israelites saw it, they said to each other, "What is it?" They
> didn't know what it was.

36

Moses said to them, "This is the bread that the LORD has
given you to eat. This is what the LORD has commanded:
'Collect as much of it as each of you can eat, one omer
per person. You may collect for the number of people in
your household.'" The Israelites did as Moses said, some
collecting more, some less. But when they measured it out
by the omer, the ones who had collected more had nothing left over, and the ones who had collected less had no
shortage. Everyone collected just as much as they could eat.
Moses said to them, "Don't keep any of it until morning."
But they didn't listen to Moses. Some kept part of it until
morning, but it became infested with worms and stank.
Moses got angry with them. Every morning they gathered
it, as much as each person could eat. But when the sun
grew hot, it melted away.

John 6:30-35

They asked, "What miraculous sign will you do, that we
can see and believe you? What will you do? Our ancestors
ate manna in the wilderness, just as it is written, He gave
them bread from heaven to eat."

Jesus told them, "I assure you, it wasn't Moses who gave
the bread from heaven to you, but my Father gives you the
true bread from heaven. The bread of God is the one who
comes down from heaven and gives life to the world."

They said, "Sir, give us this bread all the time!"

Jesus replied, "I am the bread of life. Whoever comes to
me will never go hungry, and whoever believes in me will
never be thirsty."

James 2:14-17

My brothers and sisters, what good is it if people say they
have faith but do nothing to show it? Claiming to have

faith can't save anyone, can it? Imagine a brother or sister who is naked and never has enough food to eat. What if one of you said, "Go in peace! Stay warm! Have a nice meal!"? What good is it if you don't actually give them what their body needs? In the same way, faith is dead when it doesn't result in faithful activity.

OPENING YOUR SESSION

Welcome participants. Ask volunteers who attended previous sessions to talk briefly about how insights they've gained from the study so far have been shaping their prayer and work (*ora et labora*).

Consult the list of questions about the Lord's Prayer your group made in Session 1. Ask whether participants now have answers or insights about these questions to offer the group.

Invite participants to divide a piece of paper into two columns. In one column, they should write everything they ate yesterday; in the second, how much each item cost (actual amount or best guesstimate). Tell participants you will not be asking them to share their responses with anyone else. Suggest quick internet searches can help them find or estimate prices. Tell participants to total the amount of money.

Tell participants that, according to the Bureau of Labor Statistics, the average U.S. household spends $7,203 on food per year. Divided by 365 days, that amount is $19.73 a day. Read the figures about poverty Adam Hamilton includes from the U.S. Department of Health and Human Services. Point out a total income of $12,000 in a year of 365 days is $32.88 per day, and $25,000 divided equally among four people for 365 days is $17.12 per day. Write these daily amounts on newsprint or markerboard, and/or share them in chat.

Ask participants to review their charts and circle what they ate that they consider essential. Ask them to think about (they need not respond aloud) how much of their overall eating was essential eating and to compare their spending on food to the daily amounts discussed earlier. Invite volunteers to talk briefly about what completing this activity leads them to think and feel (be ready to offer your own response to spark discussion).

Tell participants Hamilton says the word usually translated "daily" in the Lord's Prayer means "that which is needed for us to be" or "that which is essential." Read aloud from *The Lord's Prayer*: "When I pray the Lord's Prayer, I do so as one who has food in the cupboard. . . . But there are many who pray this prayer for whom this petition is, quite literally, a request for God to help them to have enough to eat." Tell participants they will, in this session, explore how God answers this petition for all who pray it.

Pray aloud this prayer or one in your own words:

Loving and life-giving God, you placed humanity in a world full of food. You sent bread from heaven to feed your people Israel in the wilderness. You sent your Son to be the Bread of Heaven for those who believe. By your Spirit, teach us in this time of study how you are still feeding people who hunger today, and show us how you choose to satisfy their hunger and thirst through us. **Amen.**

WATCH *THE LORD'S PRAYER* VIDEO

Play *The Lord's Prayer* video for Session 3 using your DVD player or stream with Amplify Media. When the session has finished, invite volunteers to lift up one or two key ideas that stood out in the video.

As you continue your discussion of the Lord's Prayer below, refer to the video as well as to chapter 3 of Hamilton's book and the Scripture passages.

REMEMBERING MANNA IN THE DESERT

Read aloud from *The Lord's Prayer*: "Unlike for the Israelites who found manna on the ground when they arose each day, God doesn't rain down food on our front lawn today." Suggest that reading the story of the manna can nevertheless help us more fully appreciate the Lord's Prayer's petition for daily bread.

Invite a volunteer to read aloud Exodus 16:14-21. Discuss:

- What does this story show us about God's care for the Israelites? If, as Hamilton writes, "God doesn't rain down food" now, what can the story show us about God's care today?
- Manna gets its name from the people's failure to recognize it for what it is (verse 15). When and how, if ever, do you and/or your congregation fail to recognize what God provides for survival? How can we train ourselves to recognize God-given "manna" in its many forms?
- What happens when the people try to gather more manna than they need? How, if ever, have you seen literal or figurative rot when people (including, perhaps sometimes, you and your congregation) have tried to hoard more of what God gives for survival than is needed?
- How can this story motivate generosity among God's people?

THINKING ABOUT JESUS AS BREAD OF LIFE

"Throughout Scripture," Hamilton notes, "bread is [also] a metaphor for far more than food." Recruit three volunteers to read aloud John 6:30-35, taking the roles of the narrator, the crowd, and Jesus. Discuss:

- Who are the people asking Jesus for a "miraculous sign," and why (see also 6:1-15, 26-29)?
- Why does Jesus emphasize the ultimate source of the manna the Israelites ate?
- What does Jesus mean when he calls himself "the bread of life"?
- "Jesus knew that we can have all the bread that we want," writes Hamilton, "and yet be spiritually starved, just as

we can have all the wealth that we could hope for, yet still be impoverished." When, if ever, have you felt "spiritually starved"? What or who has fed or feeds that hunger, and how?

- Noting the Fourth Gospel has no story about Jesus instituting the Eucharist, Hamilton states, "John intends for his readers to think about the bread and wine of Holy Communion here." How does or how could reflecting on Jesus as the Bread of Life bring deeper meaning to your experience of Communion?

- Hamilton reminds readers that the Bread of Life also provided "real food for hungry people." How do we remember that Jesus can meet our deepest needs without minimizing his concern for people's immediate, physical needs—a concern he calls us to share?

GENEROUSLY ANSWERING OTHERS' PRAYERS FOR BREAD

Recruit a volunteer to read aloud James 2:14-17. Discuss:

- When is faith dead, according to James?
- Have you or has someone you know ever experienced a situation like the hypothetical one James describes? Were you or the other person the one in need, or the one offering only words? What happened?
- Hamilton points to his congregation's work collecting food, delivering nutritious snacks to children in low-income households, sponsoring children, and more as ways they answer the Lord's Prayer's petition for bread for other people. What do or could you and your congregation do, specifically, to be the answer to someone else's prayer for daily bread?

CLOSING YOUR SESSION

Ask volunteers to talk about one specific way they plan to show generosity to someone in need before the next session. Be ready to start discussion by sharing your own plan.

Close by inviting participants to pray together the version of the Lord's Prayer with which they are most familiar.

Option:

Invite someone from a community agency, faith-based ministry, or other organization who knows about food insecurity in your community to speak with your group, including about ways your group can help them meet your neighbors' needs for daily bread.

SESSION 4

FORGIVE...AS WE FORGIVE

SESSION GOALS

Through this session's Scripture readings, discussion, reflection, and prayer, participants will:

- Define forgiveness, clarifying what the concept does and does not mean.
- Interpret two of Jesus's parables, found in Luke 18:10-14 and Matthew 18:21-35, dealing with God's extending of and our response to forgiveness.
- Identify at least one way in which they can extend forgiveness.

BIBLICAL FOUNDATIONS

Luke 18:10-14

> *[Jesus said,] "Two people went up to the temple to pray. One was a Pharisee and the other a tax collector. The Pharisee stood and prayed about himself with these words,*

43

'God, I thank you that I'm not like everyone else—crooks,
evildoers, adulterers—or even like this tax collector. I fast
twice a week. I give a tenth of everything I receive.' But
the tax collector stood at a distance. He wouldn't even lift
his eyes to look toward heaven. Rather, he struck his chest
and said, 'God, show mercy to me, a sinner.' I tell you, this
person went down to his home justified rather than the
Pharisee. All who lift themselves up will be brought low,
and those who make themselves low will be lifted up."

Matthew 18:21-35

Then Peter said to Jesus, "Lord, how many times should I
forgive my brother or sister who sins against me? Should
I forgive as many as seven times?"

Jesus said, "Not just seven times, but rather as many as
seventy-seven times. Therefore, the kingdom of heaven
is like a king who wanted to settle accounts with his
servants. When he began to settle accounts, they brought to
him a servant who owed him ten thousand bags of gold.
Because the servant didn't have enough to pay it back, the
master ordered that he should be sold, along with his wife
and children and everything he had, and that the proceeds
should be used as payment. But the servant fell down,
kneeled before him, and said, 'Please, be patient with me,
and I'll pay you back.' The master had compassion on that
servant, released him, and forgave the loan.

"When that servant went out, he found one of his fellow
servants who owed him one hundred coins. He grabbed
him around the throat and said, 'Pay me back what you
owe me.'

"Then his fellow servant fell down and begged him, 'Be
patient with me, and I'll pay you back.' But he refused.
Instead, he threw him into prison until he paid back his
debt.

"When his fellow servants saw what happened, they were deeply offended. They came and told their master all that happened. His master called the first servant and said, 'You wicked servant! I forgave you all that debt because you appealed to me. Shouldn't you also have mercy on your fellow servant, just as I had mercy on you?' His master was furious and handed him over to the guard responsible for punishing prisoners, until he had paid the whole debt.

"My heavenly Father will also do the same to you if you don't forgive your brother or sister from your heart."

OPENING YOUR SESSION

Welcome participants. Ask volunteers who attended previous sessions to talk briefly about how insights they've gained from the study so far have been shaping their prayer and work (*ora et labora*).

Consult the list of questions about the Lord's Prayer your group made in Session 1. Ask whether participants now have answers or insights about these questions to offer the group.

Ask: Which of these three translations of the petition in the Lord's Prayer about forgiveness did they first learn? Which version do they use most regularly? Is it the version they prefer? Why or why not?

- sins / those who sin against us
- trespasses / those who trespass against us
- debts / our debtors

Adam Hamilton writes that *forgiveness* is "a word we all think we know and understand, but it's helpful to clarify what we do and don't mean by" it. Ask volunteers to define *forgiveness*. Write responses on newsprint or markerboard. Encourage participants to refer back to these responses as, in this session, your group explores the petition about asking for forgiveness and extending it to others.

Pray aloud this prayer or one in your own words:

Merciful God, when we were dead in sin, you sent your Son to reconcile us to yourself. May your Spirit of love fill our listening and speaking today, that we may receive your gift of forgiveness more fully and extend it more freely, for the sake of our Savior, Jesus Christ. **Amen.**

WATCH *THE LORD'S PRAYER* VIDEO

Play *The Lord's Prayer* video for Session 4 using your DVD player or stream with Amplify Media. When the session has finished, invite volunteers to lift up one or two key ideas that stood out in the video.

As you continue your discussion of the Lord's Prayer below, refer to the video as well as to chapter 4 of Hamilton's book and the Scripture passages.

CLARIFYING WHAT FORGIVENESS MEANS—AND DOESN'T

Now that your group has attempted to define what forgiveness *is*, read these statements from Adam Hamilton about what it *isn't*, and invite volunteers to respond to each.

- Forgiveness doesn't mean "all the consequences of our sin have been released."
- Forgiveness "does not excuse the action of the one who wronged us."
- "Forgiveness is also not reconciliation with the other, though reconciliation sometimes occurs after forgiveness."
- "Forgiveness is not forgetting, but forgiveness is releasing our resentment, our visions of retribution, our bitterness and hate."

Read aloud or summarize how Hamilton uses a bag of rocks as an illustration when he preaches about forgiveness. Ask:

- Which part of Hamilton's illustration connects most powerfully with you? Why?

- ◊ the weight of sin, guilt, and shame
- ◊ the relief of remorse and repentance
- ◊ the weight of holding on to bitterness and resentment
- ◊ the relief of letting go.
- How are God's forgiveness of us and our forgiveness of others alike and different?
- How would you illustrate forgiveness in a concrete way? (*Optional*: Challenge participants to sketch an actual illustration of forgiveness on scratch paper to show the group.)

READING A PARABLE ABOUT REPENTANCE

Read aloud from *The Lord's Prayer*: "So much of Jesus's life and ministry was devoted to teaching, and offering, forgiveness."

Recruit three volunteers—the narrator (Jesus), Pharisee, and tax collector—to read aloud Luke 18:10-14, one of Jesus's parables focused on forgiveness. Discuss:

- What does this story tell us about our experience of God's forgiveness?
- "The tax collector went away justified," writes Hamilton, "not because of his righteous acts, but because of his humble expression of penitence and his longing for God's mercy." Is longing for God's mercy prerequisite for receiving it? Why or why not?
- What do you imagine motivates the Pharisee to pray as he does? How, if at all, do his motives affect the value of his prayer, fasting, and charitable giving? How, if at all, have you felt and dealt with such motives in your experience?
- First-century Jews in Judea often saw Pharisees as models of righteous behavior (Matthew 5:20; 23:1-3), and tax collectors as collaborators with the Roman government who got rich at their own people's expense (Luke 19:7-8).

How might those who first heard this story have reacted
to it?

- How do you imagine Jesus would tell this story in your
congregation or community to communicate its message?
Why?

READING A PARABLE
ABOUT SHOWING MERCY

Recruit six volunteers to read aloud Matthew 18:21-35: the
narrator, Peter, Jesus, the king, and his two servants. Discuss:

- Hamilton states that the king in Jesus's story performs "an
extraordinary gesture" for the servant in debt. What is it,
and what makes it extraordinary?
- What makes the first servant's subsequent behavior toward
his fellow servant surprising?
- What do you think about the king's final action toward
the first servant?
- How does Jesus apply his parable to our relationship
with God? How does his discussion with Peter before the
parable shape your understanding of the story?
- Which character in Jesus's story do you imagine yourself
as? How, if at all, would you hear the story differently if
you imagined yourself as one of the other characters?
- When was a time someone has showed you extraordinary
mercy? When have you showed such mercy to someone
else?
- As do the forgiveness petition and Matthew 6:14-15,
Jesus's words in Matthew 18:35 directly link, as Hamilton
writes, "the grace we ask for to the grace we are willing to
show toward others." How do you understand this link?
- "To Jesus's first-century hearers," writes Hamilton, "most
of whom owed debt and knew the consequences of

nonpayment, thinking of their sins as debts and others who sinned against them as debtors was powerful and illuminating." How powerful do you think this economic image of sin is in our century, and why?

- According to Hamilton, some wonder if Jesus's use of a financial image for sin "is also meant to lead us to practice economic forgiveness when we are owed money by someone who is struggling to repay." What do you think, and why?
- When might we need to show mercy and forgiveness to ourselves?

CLOSING YOUR SESSION

Ask volunteers to talk about one specific way they plan to extend forgiveness, to others or to themselves, before the next session. Be ready to start discussion by sharing your own plan.

Close by inviting participants to pray together the version of the Lord's Prayer with which they are most familiar.

Note:

Mention throughout your discussion, as Hamilton does throughout his, that forgiveness does not mean willingly enduring or returning to abusive situations. Should your discussion bring abusive situations to light, be prepared to help people find support and resources in your area. Some numbers and websites you may find helpful:

- **National Domestic Violence Hotline–**
  1-800-799-SAFE (7233);
  https://www.thehotline.org/
- **Victim Connect Resource Center–**
  855-4-VICTIM (855-484-2846);
  https://victimconnect.org/resources/national-hotlines/

SESSION 5

LEAD US,
NOT INTO TEMPTATION

SESSION GOALS

Through this session's Scripture readings, discussion, reflection, and prayer, participants will:

- Reflect privately on their own experiences of being tempted.
- Explore Scripture's "archetypal story of temptation" in Genesis 3, and Jesus's experience of temptation in Matthew 4.
- Discuss how the "armor of God" described in Ephesians 6 can help us withstand temptation.

BIBLICAL FOUNDATIONS

Genesis 3:1-6

> *The snake was the most intelligent of all the wild animals that the LORD God had made. He said to the woman,*

"Did God really say that you shouldn't eat from any tree in the garden?"

The woman said to the snake, "We may eat the fruit of the garden's trees but not the fruit of the tree in the middle of the garden. God said, 'Don't eat from it, and don't touch it, or you will die.'"

The snake said to the woman, "You won't die! God knows that on the day you eat from it, you will see clearly and you will be like God, knowing good and evil." The woman saw that the tree was beautiful with delicious food and that the tree would provide wisdom, so she took some of its fruit and ate it, and also gave some to her husband, who was with her, and he ate it.

Matthew 4:1-11

Then the Spirit led Jesus up into the wilderness so that the devil might tempt him. After Jesus had fasted for forty days and forty nights, he was starving. The tempter came to him and said, "Since you are God's Son, command these stones to become bread."

Jesus replied, "It's written, People won't live only by bread, but by every word spoken by God."

After that the devil brought him into the holy city and stood him at the highest point of the temple. He said to him, "Since you are God's Son, throw yourself down; for it is written, I will command my angels concerning you, and they will take you up in their hands so that you won't hit your foot on a stone."

Jesus replied, "Again it's written, Don't test the Lord your God."

Then the devil brought him to a very high mountain and showed him all the kingdoms of the world and their glory. He said, "I'll give you all these if you bow down and worship me."

Jesus responded, "Go away, Satan, because it's written, You will worship the Lord your God and serve only him." The devil left him, and angels came and took care of him.

Ephesians 6:11-17

Put on God's armor so that you can make a stand against the tricks of the devil. We aren't fighting against human enemies but against rulers, authorities, forces of cosmic darkness, and spiritual powers of evil in the heavens. Therefore, pick up the full armor of God so that you can stand your ground on the evil day and after you have done everything possible to still stand. So stand with the belt of truth around your waist, justice as your breastplate, and put shoes on your feet so that you are ready to spread the good news of peace. Above all, carry the shield of faith so that you can extinguish the flaming arrows of the evil one. Take the helmet of salvation and the sword of the Spirit, which is God's word.

ADDITIONAL PREPARATION FOR SESSION 5

- **Optional:** Gather video of "Trust in Me" from *The Jungle Book* (Disney, 1967) and a recording of "Precious Lord, Take My Hand."

OPENING YOUR SESSION

Welcome participants. Ask volunteers who attended previous sessions to talk briefly about how insights they've gained from the study so far have been shaping their prayer and work (*ora et labora*).

Consult the list of questions about the Lord's Prayer your group made in Session 1. Ask whether participants now have new answers or insights about these questions to offer the group.

Tell participants Adam Hamilton mentions, in chapter 5, a scene in the animated Disney film *The Jungle Book* in which the python Kaa hypnotizes Mowgli, intending to devour him. Optional: Watch this scene (a musical number entitled "Trust in Me") together. Discuss:

- "Hypnosis is an apt metaphor for temptation," writes Hamilton; "it's as if we fall under a spell and become susceptible to suggestion." How helpfully do you think *The Jungle Book* scene illustrates the experience of being tempted? Why?
- Hamilton writes "The question is not whether we will be tempted, but how we will respond when temptation comes." What have you discovered, in your own or others' experience, are effective ways to resist temptation?
- How well does our society as a whole resist temptation? Why?
- Has the petition that God "lead us not into temptation" confused you, as it confused the member of Hamilton's congregation? For what do you think we are asking God in this petition of the Lord's Prayer?

According to Hamilton, "God does not tempt us to do what is wrong. God wants to encourage us to do what is right." The question posed by this petition is: Who will you invite to lead you? Tell participants this session will help your group explore and answer that question.

Pray aloud this prayer or one in your own words:

High and holy God, you have set the way of life before us, but too often we allow ourselves to be led, and lead ourselves, into ways of physical and spiritual harm, even death. By your Spirit, help us focus on your word and will in this time together, that we may more faithfully obey and follow you, for the sake of him who was tempted as we are, yet without sin, Jesus Christ. **Amen.**

WATCH *THE LORD'S PRAYER* VIDEO

Play *The Lord's Prayer* video for Session 5 using your DVD player or stream with Amplify Media. When the session has finished, invite volunteers to lift up one or two key ideas that stood out in the video.

As you continue your discussion of the Lord's Prayer below, refer to the video as well as to chapter 5 of Hamilton's book and the Scripture passages.

TO BE HUMAN IS TO BE TEMPTED

Hamilton calls Genesis 3 "the archetypal story of temptation," meaning it speaks to the universal human experience of being tempted. Recruit three volunteers to read aloud Genesis 3:1-6 (the narrator, the serpent, the woman). Discuss:

- What does the serpent tempt the woman to do? Why does the woman do it? Why do you think the story describes the woman's motives but not the serpent's?

- "The serpent," writes Hamilton, "was great at rationalizing and making arguments for doing the very thing God had told Adam and Eve not to do." How have you experienced humans being "great" at rationalizing sin? Why doesn't God's gift of intelligence guard us more surely against temptation?

- In Genesis 3:11-13, the man blames the woman and the woman blames the serpent for their violation of God's commandment. What makes it so difficult to shoulder the blame for our failures to escape temptation?

- Later tradition identifies the serpent as Satan, but the story does not. What are some "serpents" in our world today that entice us to do what we shouldn't do?

TEMPTED AS WE ARE, BUT WITHOUT SIN

Recruit three volunteers to read aloud Matthew 4:1-11 (the narrator, the devil, Jesus). Discuss:

- Does the Spirit lead Jesus into temptation (verse 1)? Why or why not?
- How tempting do you think Jesus found each of the devil's efforts, and why?
- Hamilton notes, "Just because someone quotes Scripture [as the devil quotes it to Jesus] does not mean they are leading you in the right path." When, if ever, have you discovered this truth for yourself?
- How do you imagine that Jesus's experience of temptation informed what he taught his disciples to pray about temptation?
- How much comfort have you taken in knowing Jesus experienced temptation? (See also Hebrews 2:18; 4:14-16.)

PUTTING ON THE ARMOR OF GOD

Recruit a volunteer to read aloud Ephesians 6:11-17. Discuss:

- How helpful or unhelpful do you find the idea of the devil as an explanation for temptation, and why?
- How does each item in the metaphorical "armor of God" help us withstand temptation?
- Which piece of this spiritual equipment do you rely on most, and how?
- Which piece might you be well equipped to provide others, and why?
- Hamilton asks, "Where are the places where you see Christians embracing darkness instead of light today?" What are those places for you, and why? How do you respond when you see Christians "embracing darkness"?

- How does (or how ought) verse 12's insistence that our battle is not against human enemies shape the way we relate to others in our polarized society and polarized churches?
- What conclusions can we draw from the fact that the only offensive weapon in God's armor is "the sword of the Spirit, which is God's word" (verse 17)?

CLOSING YOUR SESSION

Ask volunteers to talk about one specific area of their life, small or large, in which they plan to invite or re-invite God to lead them before the next session. Be ready to start discussion by sharing your own plan.

Close by inviting participants to pray together the version of the Lord's Prayer with which they are most familiar.

Option:

Read or sing together Thomas Dorsey's hymn, "Precious Lord, Take My Hand," which Hamilton mentions, or listen to a recording of it together as part of your opening or closing prayer.

Note:

This session plan does not require or expect you to ask participants to talk publicly about their specific, personal temptations. Should some choose to, thank them for their honesty. As appropriate, offer whatever support you and your group can to help the person find resources for resisting temptation more effectively. Remind participants that addiction issues involve temptation but are also diseases that can be treated.

SESSION 6

FOR THINE IS THE KINGDOM, POWER, AND GLORY

SESSION GOALS

Through this session's Scripture readings, discussion, reflection, and prayer, participants will:

- Explore the place and power of praising God in our prayer by examining King David's prayer in 1 Chronicles 29.
- Compare and contrast the disciples' and Jesus's understandings of kingdom, power, and glory in Luke 22:24-30.
- Identify and discuss practical implications of the doxology that ends the Lord's Prayer.
- Evaluate this study's impact on their own prayer and work (*ora et labora*).

BIBLICAL FOUNDATIONS

1 Chronicles 29:10-19

> *Then David blessed the LORD before the whole assembly:*

Blessed are you, LORD,
> *God of our ancestor Israel,*
>> *forever and always.*

To you, LORD, belong greatness and power,
> *honor, splendor, and majesty,*
>> *because everything in heaven and on earth*
>> *belongs to you.*

Yours, LORD, is the kingship,
> *and you are honored as head of all.*

You are the source of wealth and honor,
> *and you rule over all.*

In your hand are strength and might,
> *and it is in your power to magnify and*
> *strengthen all.*

And now, our God, we thank you
> *and praise your glorious name.*

Who am I,
> *and who are my people,*
>> *that we should be able to offer so willingly?*

Since everything comes from you,
> *we have given you that which comes from your*
> *own hand.*

To be sure, we are like all our ancestors,
> *immigrants without permanent homes.*

Our days are like a shadow on the ground,
> *and there's no hope.*

*LORD, our God, all this abundance that we have provided
to build you a temple for your holy name comes from your
hand and belongs to you. Since I know, my God, that
you examine the mind and take delight in honesty, I have
freely given all these things with the highest of motives.
And now I've been delighted to see your people here
offering so willingly to you.*

> LORD, *God of our ancestors Abraham, Isaac, and Israel,*
> *keep these thoughts in the mind of your people forever, and*
> *direct their hearts toward you.*
>
> *As for Solomon my son, give him the wholehearted devo-*
> *tion to keep your commands, laws, and regulations—ob-*
> *serving all of them—and to build the temple that I have*
> *prepared.*

Luke 22:24-30

> *An argument broke out among the disciples over which*
> *one of them should be regarded as the greatest.*
>
> *But Jesus said to them, "The kings of the Gentiles rule*
> *over their subjects, and those in authority over them are*
> *called 'friends of the people.' But that's not the way it will*
> *be with you. Instead, the greatest among you must become*
> *like a person of lower status and the leader like a servant.*
> *So which one is greater, the one who is seated at the table*
> *or the one who serves at the table? Isn't it the one who is*
> *seated at the table? But I am among you as one who serves.*
>
> *"You are the ones who have continued with me in my*
> *trials. And I confer royal power on you just as my Father*
> *granted royal power to me. Thus you will eat and drink*
> *at my table in my kingdom, and you will sit on thrones*
> *overseeing the twelve tribes of Israel."*

OPENING YOUR SESSION

Welcome participants. Tell those familiar with the format of previous sessions you will ask for *ora et labora* insights and answers to the group's list of questions at the end of this session.

Ask volunteers to talk about a spontaneous expression of praise they have witnessed (examples might include: a standing ovation for a performer, a crowd at a sporting event cheering a big play, someone simply taking time to praise another person). What thoughts and feelings did this expression of praise stir in them? What effects, if any, did it appear to have on the person(s) giving and receiving the praise?

Tell participants, in Adam Hamilton's words, the last line of the Lord's Prayer, or "doxology," "likely was not originally a part of the prayer that Jesus taught, though by the end of the first century Christians were reciting this or something very close to it as a shout of praise in response to the prayer." Tell participants this session will explore how this doxology can shape our experience of the Lord's Prayer and our relationships with God and other people.

Pray aloud this prayer or one in your own words:

Blessed are you, God of Israel and Father of our Lord Jesus Christ, forever and always. Again send your Spirit to teach and train us in prayer, and indeed to pray for us, that we may more fully offer ourselves to you, for the sake of him who offered himself for us and the world, our Savior Jesus Christ. **Amen.**

WATCH *THE LORD'S PRAYER* VIDEO

Play *The Lord's Prayer* video for Session 6 using your DVD player or stream with Amplify Media. When the session has finished, invite volunteers to lift up one or two key ideas that stood out in the video.

As you continue your discussion of the Lord's Prayer below, refer to the video as well as to chapter 6 of Hamilton's book and the Scripture passages.

DISCUSSING KING DAVID'S DOXOLOGY

According to Hamilton, the prayer King David prays as the people of Israel make offerings for the future construction of the Temple, inspired the doxology that now concludes the Lord's Prayer. Recruit a volunteer to read aloud this prayer, in 1 Chronicles 29:10-19. Discuss:

- David's prayer begins with extensive praise of God (verses 10-13) and ends with petitions (verses 18-19). How do these positions and proportions of praise and petition compare to your own prayers? to your congregation's?

- What reasons does David mention for praising God? Which, if any, of these reasons resonates most strongly with you, and why?
- How does David's praise of God present a clear picture of his relationship to God (verses 11-12)? the whole people's relationship to God (verses 14-15)? When, if ever, has your own expression of praise clarified your relationship to God?
- David stresses the importance of honesty before God (verse 17). How do you keep yourself honest before God in your prayers?

GOD'S IS THE KINGDOM, POWER, AND GLORY

"Once more," writes Hamilton, "when we come to the doxology to the Lord's Prayer, we are choosing Thy and Thine instead of my and mine." Recruit a volunteer to read aloud Luke 22:24-30. Discuss:

- What does the disciples' argument reveal they think about the concepts of kingdom, power, and glory? What does Jesus's response show he thinks?
- Throughout his life and ministry, how was Jesus among his disciples and other people "as one who serves" (verse 27)?
- What is the connection between sharing in Jesus's trials and receiving "royal power" (verse 29)? How can and do Christians today share in Jesus's trials? Does Jesus's promise to his first followers apply also to his followers today? Why or why not?
- Hamilton writes "when we lose our lives for God's sake, when we lay down our crowns, when we stop craving power, and when we give God the glory instead of seeking

it for ourselves, we live large, magnanimous lives." Who are some people you know or know of who live or lived such lives?

- Hamilton calls the doxology in the Lord's Prayer "a pledge of our allegiance to God's kingdom, power, and glory." How do Christians determine whether and when their allegiance to other powers is in conflict with their allegiance to God?

- Hamilton states that pledging our allegiance to God means "we must ask probing questions of our nation and of our leaders." What policies, laws, and positions do you think Christians in America today need to be asking probing questions about, and why?

- "Each of us also has power," writes Hamilton. What is a specific area of your life in which you have power? How can and will you use this power "to impact others' lives and the world around us" for God?

- Hamilton says the doxology in the Lord's Prayer helps us counter "the natural tendency in our lives to seek glory for ourselves." How much or how little do you feel this tendency, and why? Under what conditions, if any, is it acceptable for Christians to "want the credit for the good things we do"? How do we keep our prayer for God's glory from becoming a justification for denying other people the recognition and respect they deserve?

CLOSING YOUR SESSION

Ask volunteers to talk about one specific way they can use their power to glorify God in the days ahead. Be ready to start discussion by sharing your own plan.

Thank participants for their engagement with this study of *The Lord's Prayer*.

Consult the list of questions about the Lord's Prayer your group made in Session 1. Ask whether participants have any final answers or insights about these questions to offer the group.

Ask volunteers to talk briefly about the major insight they think they will take from the study that will continue to shape their prayer and work (*ora et labora*).

Close by inviting participants to pray together the version of the Lord's Prayer with which they are most familiar.

WATCH VIDEOS BASED ON *THE LORD'S PRAYER: THE MEANING AND POWER OF THE PRAYER JESUS TAUGHT* WITH ADAM HAMILTON THROUGH AMPLIFY MEDIA.

Amplify Media is a multimedia platform that delivers high quality, searchable content with an emphasis on Wesleyan perspectives for churchwide, group, or individual use on any device at any time. In a world of sometimes overwhelming choices, Amplify gives church leaders and congregants media capabilities that are contemporary, relevant, effective and, most importantly, affordable and sustainable.

With **Amplify Media** church leaders can:

• Provide a reliable source of Christian content through a Wesleyan lens for teaching, training, and inspiration in a customizable library
• Deliver their own preaching and worship content in a way the congregation knows and appreciates
• Build the church's capacity to innovate with engaging content and accessible technology
• Equip the congregation to better understand the Bible and its application
• Deepen discipleship beyond the church walls

∧ AMPLIFY. MEDIΛ

Ask your group leader or pastor about Amplify Media and sign up today at www.AmplifyMedia.com.

9 781791 021283

CPSIA information can be obtained
at www.ICGtesting.com
Printed in the USA
LVHW032229040822
724923LV00002B/10